תלתי חזירייה זעורייה

Talte Ḥaziraiyah Zəʻoraiyah
"The Three Little Pigs"

Translation into Galilean Aramaic
by Steve Caruso

This work is based upon an abridged version of *"The Story of the Three Little Pigs: With Drawings by L. Leslie Brooke,"* originally published by Frederick Warne & Co. in the late 1800s and now is in the Public Domain.

This edition is aimed towards students of the Galilean Aramaic language family and makes use of standardized orthographical conventions to ease reading. The text is trilinear and includes 1) the Galilean Aramaic text with Palestinian Vocalization (see the Lexicon and Appendices for more information), 2) a transliteration to indicate pronunciation, and 3) a plain English translation.

Rogue
Leaf
press

Non-Public Domain Portions
© 2014 RogueLeaf Press

First edition.

לצרי ראות לוהן וילהנה בקמר בל ירם

To my children, that they always have a story to read.

The Three Little Pigs

אֵי זֻמָן הַוֻת חֲזִירָה סַוַח עִם תְּלַת חֲזִירִין זְעוֹרִין

/ḥaḏ zəman həwaṯ ḥazirah savah ʿam təlaṯ ḥazirin zəʿorin/

Once upon a time there was an old Sow with three Little Pigs.

בָּגִין לֵית לָהּ מְפַרְנְסָה לְהוֹן

/bəḡin leṯ lah məfarnasah ləhon/

Because she had not enough to keep them,

הִיא שַׁדְרַת לְהוֹן לְמֶטְבַּע גַּדֵיהוֹן

/hiʾ šaḏraṯ ləhon ləmeṯbaʿ gadehon/

she sent them out to seek their fortunes.

אֲזַל קַדְמָיָא וְאַשְׁכַּח בַּרְנָשׁ עִם מִישְׁרָה דְּתָבָן

/ʾəzal qadmaiya wə-ʾaškaḥ barnaš ʿm misrah də-ṯəvan/

The first went and found a Man with a bundle of straw,

וַאֲמַר לֵיהּ

/wa-ʾəmar leh/

and said to him,

בְּבָעוּ מָרִי הַב לִי הָדֵין תַּבְנָה דְּאֶעֱבֵד בֵּיתִי

/bəvaʿu mari hav li hadən təvnah də-ʾəʿbeḏ baiṯi/

"Please, Sir, give me that straw that I may build my house";

3

וְיָהַב בַּרְנַשׁ לֵיהּ תַּבְנָה

/wə-yəhav barnaš leh təvnah/

and the Man gave him the straw,

וַעֲבַד חֲזִירָה זְעוֹרָה בַּיְתֵהּ עֲמֵהּ

/wa-ʿəved ḥazirah zəʿorah baiteh ʿəmeh/

and the little Pig built his house with it.

וַאֲתָה דֵּיב וּנְקַשׁ עַל תַּרְעָה וַאֲמַר

/wa-ʾətah dev wa-nəqaš ʿəl tarʿah wa-ʾəmar/

And along came a Wolf, and he knocked at the door, and
said

חֲזִירָה זְעוֹרָה חֲזִירָה זְעוֹרָה שְׁרִי לִי מִיעוֹל

/ḥazirah zəʿorah ḥazirah zəʿorah šəri li miʿol/

"Little Pig, little Pig, let me come in."

4

וְאָתֵב חֲזִירָה
/wə-'atev ḥazirah/
And the Pig answered,

לֹא בְּשַׂעֲרַה עַל דֶקְנִי כָּלוֹם
/la' ba-śə'rah 'əl deqni kəlom/
"Not by the hair of my chinny chin chin!"

הָא אֶפַח וְאֶפַח
/ha' 'epaḥ wə-'epaḥ/
"Then I'll huff and I'll puff,

וְאָפֵל בֵּיתָךְ
/wə-'apel baitak̲/
and I'll blow your house in!"

אָזֵא הָפֵ לֵח הָפֵ חֹאָ
/wə-ha' nəfaḥ wa-nəfaḥ/
So he huffed and he puffed,

אָזֵאַ אֵתֵיל בֵּיתָה
/wə-'apel baitah/
and he blew the house in,

אָזֵאָל הָזִירֶה וְעֹרֶתֵה
/wa-'əkal ḥazirah zə'orah/
and ate up the little Pig.

6

חֲזִירָה תִנְיָנָה אַשְׁכַּח בַּרְנָשׁ עִם מִסְרָה דְּחוֹטְרִין

/ḥazirah tǝnyanah ʾaškaḥ barnaš ʿm misrah dǝ-ḥoṭrin/

The second Pig found a Man with a bundle of sticks,

וַאֲמַר לֵיהּ

/wa-ʾǝmar leh/

and he said to him,

בָּעוּ מָרִי הַב לִי הָאֵלָיִין חוֹטְרַיָה דְּאֶעְבֵּד בַּיְתִי

/bǝvaʿu mari hav li haʾelaiyin ḥoṭraiyah dǝ-ʾǝʿbed baiṭi/

"Please, Sir, give me those sticks that I may build my house";

וַיְהַב בַּרְנָשׁ לֵיהּ חוֹטְרַיָה

/wa-yǝhav barnaš leh ḥoṭraiyah/

and the Man gave him the sticks,

וַעֲבֵד חֲזִירָה זְעוֹרָה בַּיְתֵיהּ עִמְהוֹן

/wa-ʿved ḥazirah zǝʿorah baiṭeh ʿmǝhon/

and the little Pig built his house with them.

הֵיךְ קֳדָם אֲתָה דֵּיבָא וַנְקַשׁ עַל תַּרְעָה וַאֲמַר

/hek qodam ʾǝtah devah wa-nǝqaš ʿal tarʿah wa-ʾǝmar/

Like before: Along came the Wolf, and he knocked at the door, and said,

חֲזִירָה זְעוֹרָה חֲזִירָה זְעוֹרָה שְׁרִי לִי מִעוֹל

/ḥazirah zǝʿorah ḥazirah zǝʿorah šǝri li miʿol/

"Little Pig, little Pig, let me come in."

וֹאתֵב חֲזִירָה

/wə-'aṭev ḥazirah/

And the Pig answered,

לֹא בַּשְּׂעְרָה עֵל דֶקְנִי כְלוֹם

/la' ba-śə'rah 'əl deqni kəlom/

"Not by the hair of my chinny chin chin!"

הָא אֵפָּח וֹאֵפָּח

/ha' epaḥ wə-'epaḥ/

"Then I'll huff and I'll puff,

וֹאַפֵּל בֵּיתָך

/wə-'apel baiṯak/

and I'll blow your house in!"

וֹהָא נְפָח וַנְפָח

/wə-ha' nəfaḥ wa-nəfaḥ/

So he huffed and he puffed,

וֹאַפֵּל בֵּיתָה

/wə-'apel baiṯah/

and he blew the house in,

וֹאֱכַל חֲזִירָה זְעוֹרָה

/wa-'əkal ḥazirah zə'orah/

and ate up the little Pig.

8

חֲזִירָה תְּלִיתָיְיה אַשְׁכַּח בַּרְנָשׁ עִם מִיסְרַה דְּלִבְנִין

/ḥazirah təliṯaiyah ʾaškaḥ barnaš ʾəm misrah də-levnin/

The third Pig found a Man with a bundle of bricks,

וַאֲמַר לֵיהּ

/wa-ʾəmar leh/

and he said to him,

בֵּיתִי לְמֶעְבַּד הָאֵלֵין לְבֵנַיָּה הַב לִי מָרִי בָּעוּ

/bəva'u mari hav li ha'elaiyin levnaiyah də-'ə'bed baiti/

"Please, Sir, give me those bricks that I may build my house";

וִיהַב בַּרְנָשׁ לֵיהּ לְבֵנַיָּה

/wə-yəhav barnaš leh levnaiyah/

and the Man gave him the bricks,

וַעֲבַד חֲזִירָה זְעוֹרָה בֵּיתֵיהּ עֲמֵהוֹן

/wa-'aved ḥazirah zə'orah baiteh 'əməhen/

and the little Pig built his house with them.

הֵיךְ מַה זִמְנַיָּא תַּרְתֵּין קֳדָם

/hek mah zimnaiyah traiynah qodam/

Like the two times before,

אָתָה דֵּיבָא וּנְקַשׁ עַל תַּרְעָא וַאֲמַר

/'ətah devah wa-nəqaš 'al tar'a' wa-'əmar/

Along came the Wolf, and he knocked at the door, and said,

חֲזִירָה זְעוֹרָה חֲזִירָה זְעוֹרָה שְׁרִי לִי מֵיעוֹל

/ḥazirah zə'orah ḥazirah zə'orah šəri li mi'ol/

"Little Pig, little Pig, let me come in."

וֹאתֵב חֲזִירָה

/wə-'atev ḥazirah/

And the Pig answered,

לֹא בַּשַּׂעְרָה עַל דִקְנִי כְּלוֹם

/la' ba-śə'rah 'əl deqni kəlom/

"Not by the hair of my chinny chin chin!"

הָא אִיפַח וֹאִיפַח

/ha' 'epaḥ wə-'epaḥ/

"Then I'll huff and I'll puff,

וֹאַפֵּל בֵּיתָךְ

/wə-'apel baitak/

and I'll blow your house in!"

וֹהָא נְפַח וַנְפַח

/wə-ha' nəfaḥ wa-nəfaḥ/

So he huffed and he puffed,

בְּרַם לֵת חֵיל לֵיהּ מַפָּלָה בֵּיתָה

/bəram let ḥail leh mapalah baitah/

but he did not have the strength to blow the house in!

11

וְכָעַס דֵּיבָה סָגִין

/wa-kə'as devah səgin/

Then the Wolf was very angry,

וְאָמַר אֵחַת בְּתִכְיָה

/wa-'əmar 'eḥat bə-tefyah/

and said, "I'll come down the chimney!"

בְּרַם הֵמָה חֲזִירָה זְעוֹרָה מַה דְּעַבֵד

/bəram həmah ḥazirah zə'orah mah də-'aved/

But the Little Pig saw what was happening,

וְיָהַב קְדַר דְּמַיִין עַל נוּרָה מַשְׁלֹק

/wə-yəhav qədar də-maiyin 'əl nurah məšloq/

and put a pot of water on the fire to boil.

12

נָחַת דְּבָה
/nəḥaṯ devah/
Down went the wolf!

בְּגוֹ קְדֵרָה
/bəḡo qeḏrah/
Into the pot!

וְכֵן הֲוַת כֵּן
/wə-kən hwaṯ kən/
And that was that.

13

Lexicon

Here you will find a lexicon outlining all of the words used in this publication with basic glosses. It is meant to be a study tool to better understand the composition of the story and help with disambiguation in reading.

א

אזל (v.) - "to go"

   אזל *pe'al perf. m. 3p. s.* - "he went"

אכל (v.) - "to eat"

   אכל *pe'al perf. m. 3p. s.* - "he ate"

אמר (v.) - "to say"

   אמר *pe'al perf. m. 3p. s.* - "he said"

אתי (v.) - "to come"

   אתה *pe'al perf. m. 3p. s.* - "he came"

ב

בעו (interj.) - "please"

בגו (prep.) - "inside, within"

בגין (conj.) - "because"

בית (n.f.) - "house"

   ביתה - "the house"

   ביתי *c. 1p. s.* - "my house"

   ביתך *m. 2p. s.* - "your (m.s.) house"

   ביתיה *m. 3p. s.* - "his house"

בְּרַם (conj.) - "but, however"

בַּר נָשׁ (n./pron.) - "one, someone" - lit. *"son of man"*

א‎

גַּד (n.m.) - "luck, fortune, fate"

גַּדֵּיהוֹן (pl.) *m. 3p. pl.* - "their fortunes, their lucks, their fates"

ד‎

דֵּאב (n.m.) - "wolf"

דֵּאבָה - "the wolf"

דְּקַן (n.m.) - "chin, beard"

דְּקַנִי - "my chin"

ה‎

הָאִלֵּין (pron.) - these, those

הָדֵין (pron.) - this (m.s.)

הֲוָה (v.) - "to be"

הֲוָת *pe'al perf. f. 3p. s.* - "she/it was"

הֵיךְ (prep.) - like, as

ו‎

ז‎

זְעוֹר (adj.) - "little, small"

זְעוֹרָה (m.s.def.)

זְעוֹרִין (m.pl.indef.)

זְמַן (n.m.) - "time, particular time"

זִמְנַיָּא - "the times, the particular times"

ח‎

חַד (num.) - one

חוּטְרָא (n.m.) - "(a) stick, staff"

חוּטְרַיָּא - "the sticks"

חוּטְרִין - "sticks"

חֲזִיר (n.) - "(a) pig"

> חֲזִירָה "the pig (m.)" or "(a) sow (f.)"

> חֲזִירִין "pigs (m.)"

חֵיל (n.m.) - "(a) force, power, strength"

חֲזָא (v.) - "to see"

> חֲזָה *pe'al perf. m. 3p. s.* - "he saw"

ט

י

יְהַב (v.) - "to give" (with עַל - "to put")

> הַב *pe'al imperat. m. 2p. s.* - "give"

> יְהַב *pe'al perf. m. 3p. s.* - "he gave"

כ

כְּלוּם (pron.) - 1) "something" 2) "nothing"; when paired with לֹא as לֹא כְּלוּם 3) like the English *"(not/nothing) at all!"* when paired with לֹא or לֵית or ending a sentence that starts with לֹא or לֵית for emphasis.

כֵּן (adv.) - "thus, so"

כְּעֵס (v.) - to be angry

> כְּעֵס *pe'al perf. m. 3p. s.* - "he was angry"

ל

לְ- (prep.) - "to, for, unto"

> לַהּ "to her, her"

> לְהוֹן "to them, them (m.)"

> לִי "to me, me"

> לֵהּ "to him, him"

לֹא (adv.) - "no, not"

לְבֵנָה (n.f.) - "brick"

> לְבֵנָה - "the bricks"

לִבְנִין - "bricks"

לֵית (adv.) - "not, there is not"

מ

מָה (pron./conj.) - "what"

מַיִין (n.m.) - "water"

מְגוּדָה (n.f.) - "bundle, bunch, pile"

מָר (n.m.) - "lord, master, mister, sir"

> מָרִי *c. 1p. s.* - "my lord, my master" or as the polite "sir"

נ

נְחַת (v.) - "to go down, to descend, to fall"

> אֵיחֹת *pe'al imperf. c. 1p. s.* - "I will go down, I will descend, I will fall"

נְחַת *pe'al perf. m. 3p. s.* - "he went down, he descended, he fell"

נוּר (n.m.) - "fire"

נוּרָה - "the fire"

נְפַח (v.) - "to blow, to inflate"

> אֵיפֹּח *pe'al imperf. m. 1p. s.* - "I will blow, I will puff up"

נְפַח *pe'al perf. m. 3p. s.* - "He blew, he puffed"

נְפַל (v.) - "to fall"

> אַפֵּיל *af'el perf. m. 3p. s.* - "He threw/knocked down" OR *af'el imperf. m. 1p. s.* - "I will throw/knock down"
>
> אַפָּלָה *af'el infin.* - "to throw/knock down"

נקש (v.) - "to knock, strike, hit"

   נְקַשׁ *pe'al perf. m. 3p. s.* - "he knocked, struck, hit"

מ

מְאֹד (adv.) - "very, much, many"

ע

עֲבַד (v.) - "to do, make, happen"

   אֶעְבֵּד *pe'al imperf. c. 1p. s.* - "I will do, I will make" or "may I do, may I make"

   עֲבַד *pe'al perf. m. 3p. s.* - "he did, he made"

   עָבֵד *pe'al particp. m. s.* - "does, makes, happens" or "doing, making, happening"

עֲלַל (v.) - "to enter"

לְמֵעַל *pe'al inf.* - "to enter"

עִם (prep.) - "with"

   עִמְּהוֹן *m. 3p. pl.* - "with them (m.)"

   עִמְּהֵן *f. 3p. pl.* - "with them (f.)"

   עִמֵּהּ *m. 3p. s.* - "with him"

ב

סְבַר (v.) - "to support, to provide"

   לְסִבְרָה *pe'al infin.* - "to support, to provide"

צ

ק

קַדְמַי (num.) - "first"

   קַדְמָיְתָא (m.s.) - "the first"

קְדֵר (n.m.) - "pot"

   קְדֵרָה - "the pot"

קֳדָם (prep.) - before (space or time)

ר

שׁ

שׁדר (v.) - "to send out"

   שַׁדְּרַת pe'al perf. f. 3p. s. - "she sent"

שׁכח (v.) - "to find"

   אַשְׁכַּח af'el perf. m. 3p. s. - "he found"

שׁלק (v.) - "to cook, to boil"

   לְמִשְׁלַק pe'al infin. - "to cook, to boil"

שׁרי (v.) - "to loosen, to begin, to allow"

   שְׁרִי pe'al imperat. m. 2p. s. - "loosen, begin, allow"

שׁ

שְׂעַר (n.m.) - "hair"

   שַׂעְרָה - "the hair"

ת

תֶּבֶן (n.m.) - "straw, chaff"

   תִּבְנָא - "the straw, the chaff"

תְּבַע (v.) - "to seek, inquire"

   לְמִתְבַּע pe'al infin. - "to seek, to inquire"

תוב (v.) - "to return, answer"

   אֲתֵיב aph'el perf. m. 3p. s. - "he returned, he answered"

תְּנוּר (n.m.) - "hearth, fireplace"

   תְּנוּרָה - "the hearth, the fireplace"

תְּלִיתַי (num.) - "third"

   תְּלִיתָיָה - "the third"

תְּלָת (num.) - "three"

20

[script] (num.) - "second"

[script] - "the second"

[script] (num.) - "two"

[script] - "the two"

[script] (n.m.) - "door, gate"

[script] - "the door, the gate"

Appendix A: Transliteration

Letter:	Form:	Translit.:	Other:
'əlaf	א	'	*ə, a*
Beṯ	ב	*b*	*v*
Gəmal	ג	*g*	*ḡ*
Dəlaṯ	ד	*d*	*ḏ*
He	ה	*h*	
Wau	ו	*w*	*u, o*
Zai	ז	*z*	
Ḥeṯ	ח	*ḥ*	
Ṭeṯ	ט	*ṭ*	
Yoḏ	י	*y*	*e, i*
Kaf	כ, ך	*k*	*ḵ*
Ləmaḏ	ל	*l*	
Məm	מ, ם	*m*	
Nun	נ, ן	*n*	
Səmeḵ	ס	*s*	
'Ayin	ע	'	
Pe	פ, ף	*p*	*f*
Çade	צ, ץ	*ç*	

Letter:	Form:	Translit.:	Other:
Qof	ק	*q*	
Resh	ר	*r*	
Šin	שׁ	*š*	
Śin	שׂ	*ś*	
Tau	ת	*t*	*t̲*

Out of all of these letters, *b, v, g, d, h, w, z, y, k, l, m, n, s, p, f, r,* and *t* are pronounced as they are in English. The rest require some clarification and below are examples in General American English unless otherwise specified:

’ → (silent)

ə → <u>a</u>bove

a → h<u>o</u>t

ḡ → "gh," ami<u>g</u>o (Spanish)

d̲ → <u>th</u>e

u → r<u>u</u>de

o → <u>o</u>ver

ḥ → lo<u>ch</u> (Scottish), Ba<u>ch</u> (German)

ṭ → a hard "t"

e → h<u>ey</u>

i → thr<u>ee</u>

k̲ → like ḥ but a bit softer

‘ → a hard "uh" in the back of the throat, almost like the sound one makes before they vomit

ç → "tsh," po<u>ts</u>

q → a hard "k" in the very back of the throat

š → <u>sh</u>in

ś → a cross between the sounds of *s* and *š*

t̲ → <u>th</u>ree

Emphasis on most words falls upon on the last syllable, but where this is not the case an accent mark will be written on the appropriate vowel (e.g. *ə́, á, é, í, ó, ú*).

Examples

24

ܚܙܝܪܝܢ	=	/ḥazirin/	=	kha-zee-REEN
ܐܙܠ	=	/ʾəzal/	=	uh-ZAL
ܡܠܟܘܬܗ	=	/malkuṯah/	=	mahl-koo-THAH
ܐܢܚܢܗ	=	/ʾənáḥnah/	=	uh-NAKH-nah

Appendix B: Palestinian Vocalization

Because of the reduced vowel inventory found in Galilean Aramaic and the fact that it is found predominantly with Palestinian Aramaic and Palestinian Hebrew, Palestinian Vocalization Markings have been chosen to express vocalizations in this book. However, Palestinian Vocalization is not nearly as standardized as other vocalization systems, so the following conventions have been adopted:[1]

Vowels

א֑	אָ	א֒	א֒	א֒	א֒
ə	a	e	i	o	u
šǝwa'	paṭaḥ	*çǝre	*hǝriq	*qomaç	*qǝfuç

- א֑ - **Šǝwa'** (*Shwa*) – Two dots on the diagonal, it's like the *a* in "above"; a very short *uh*. It is represented in

---

[1] For more information about this system – both historically and this standardized form – see the forthcoming title, *"Elementary Galilean Aramaic With Exercises in Reading & Comprehension"* (RogueLeaf Press)

transliteration by *ə*.

- **א̱ - Pəṭaḥ** – A line over the top of a letter, it is an open *ah* sound. It is represented in transliteration as *a*.

- **יִ - Çəre** – Looks like a *yod* with a *shwa* over it. If it's at the beginning of a word, it's pronounced *yə-*, but everywhere else it represents an *ey* sound. In transliteration it is represented as *e*.

- **יִ - Ḥəriq** – A *yod* with two dots vertically aligned over it. It makes an *ee* sound. In transliteration it is represented by the letter *i*.

- **יִ - Qomaç** – A *wau* with three dots in a triangle over it. It makes an *oh* sound. In transliteration it is represented by the letter *o*; and finally,

- **יִ - Qəfuç** – A *wau* with two dots side-by-side over it. It makes an *oo* sound. In transliteration it is represented by the letter *u*.

Other Notations

Writing Śin

The letter **ש** *śin* is designated by writing the letter **ש** *śin* with a small **ס** *səmek* written above the leftmost arm.

Dəggesh

A *daggesh* is indicated by a small semi-circle or "L" shape written above a letter (**בּ**). It indicates either when a letter is doubled in pronunciation, or a *bəḡadkəfat* letter (**בגדכפת**) is pronounced *qəše* ("hard": *b g d k p t*) rather than *rafe* ("soft"; *v ḡ ḏ ḵ* *f ʈ*) when it falls after a vowel (ex. پَيڅِيں = *bəgin*). It also often indicates a *ə* after the letter it falls upon, provided that it does not have a vowel following it and it does not land at the end of a word.

Coming soon from RogueLeaf Press:

Elementary
Galilean
Aramaic

—With Exercises in—
Reading & Composition

Steve Caruso

Coming soon from RogueLeaf Press:

The Galilean Aramaic Lord's Prayer

And the fate of the language of Christ.

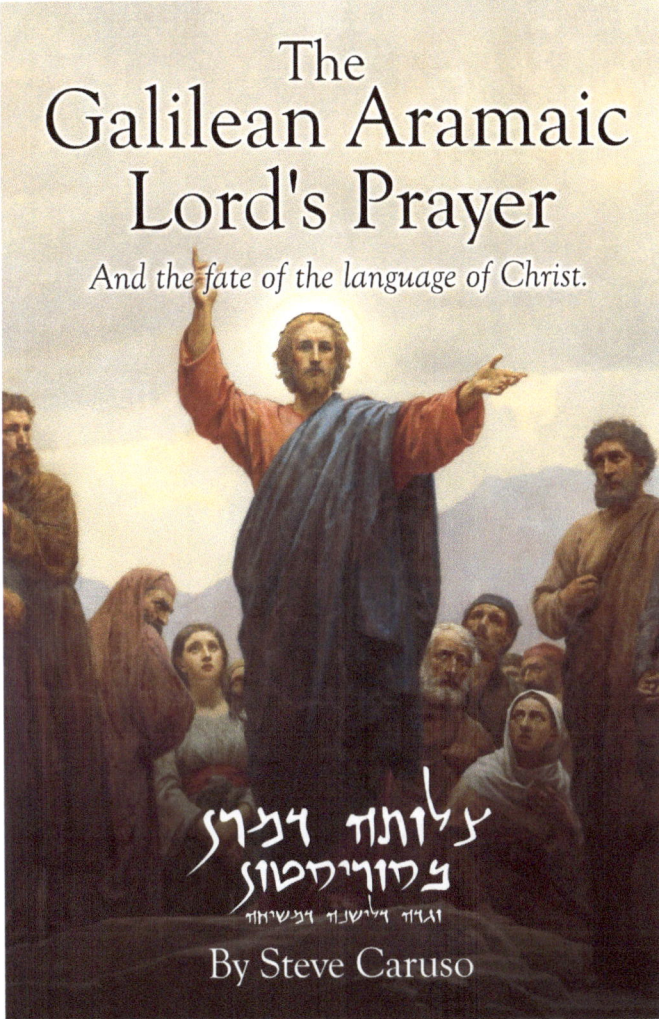

צלותא דמרן
במוריחטון
וגזר דלישנא דמשיחא

By Steve Caruso

www.ingramcontent.com/pod-product-compliance
Lightning Source LLC
LaVergne TN
LVHW010026070426
835509LV00001B/26